Silver People

Voices from the Panama Canal

Margarita Engle

Houghton Mifflin Harcourt
Boston · New York

www.hmhco.com

Text set in ITC Cheltenham Std Light.

Library of Congress Cataloging-in-Publication Data
Engle, Margarita.
Silver people : voices from the Panama Canal / Margarita Engle.
pages cm
Summary: Fourteen-year-old Mateo and other young Caribbean islanders
face discrimination, segregation, and harsh working conditions when
American recruiters lure them to the Panamanian rain forest in 1906
to build the great canal.
Includes bibliographical references.
ISBN 978-0-544-10941-4 (hardback)
1. Panama Canal (Panama)—History—Juvenile fiction. [1. Novels in
verse. 2. Panama Canal (Panama)—History—Fiction. 3. Racism—Fiction.
4. Segregation—Fiction. 5. Rain forests—Fiction.] I. Title.
PZ7.5.E54Si 2014   [Fic]—dc23   2013037485

Manufactured in the United States of America
DOC 10 9 8 7 6 5 4 3 2 1

4500457694

In honor of the islanders

who did the digging

and with love for Curtis,

who helped me explore

the butterfly forest

Panamá:

an indigenous name meaning

"land of many butterflies"

CONTENTS

THE PANAMA CRAZE

1906

MATEO from the island of Cuba

JOB HUNT

Fear is a fierce wind
that sends me reeling
down to the seashore,
where I beg for work,
any work at all,
any escape
to carry me far
from my father's
furious fists.

Sailor.
Fisherman.
Lobster trapper.
I'm willing to take any job
that floats me away
from home.

I am not an ordinary war orphan.

3

Papi is alive, but the family part

of his mind

is deeply wounded.

He drinks so much rum

that he believes I am

his enemy — a Spaniard

from the country

that lost the war

and left so many

of its soldiers

behind.

Spanish veterans

flock the seashore, begging

for the same jobs that lure me.

I'm only fourteen, but I'm strong

for a starving boy.

So I shove and curse

along with the crowd

of muscular men, all of us

equally eager to reach

a fast-talking *americano*

Panamá Canal recruiter

who promises food, houses,

and money,

so much money . . .

The recruiter shouts and pounds

his fists in the air.

His foreign accent

makes the words sound powerful

as he describes a wild jungle

where men who are hired

will dig the Eighth Wonder

of the World.

He says the canal is a challenge

worthy of Hercules,

a task for giants,

not ordinary men,

but when he unrolls a map,

Panamá is barely

a sliver.

How can such a narrow

bridge of land

be so important?

After the confusing map,

there are pamphlets with pictures

of tidy houses, the orderly dining rooms

offering comforting details

that catch my eye.

Lacy curtains and tablecloths,

flowers in vases,

plates heaped with food . . .

So much food.

Barriga llena, corazón contento.

Full belly, happy heart.

That's what Mami used to say,

before cholera claimed

her happiness

and mine.

With the flair of a magician,

the recruiter tosses two sun-shiny coins

up and down in his hand,

until the gold

American dollars

ring out like church bells

or kettledrums in a parade.

Those musical coins lure me

deeper into the crowd of pushing,

rushing, desperate, job-hungry strangers,

but as soon as I reach for the recruiter's

paper and pen, ready to sign my name

on a contract, the blond man glares

at my green eyes, brown face,

and curly hair, as if struggling

to figure out who I am.

No *cubanos,* he shouts. No islanders,

just pure Spanish,

semi-*blanco,* semi-white—

European. Civilized.

His words make no sense.

Isn't semi-white the same

as semi-dark?

So I start telling lies.

I let my skin fib.

I point out that my father

is blondish and my mother

was the tan of toasted wheat,

her hair long and silky,

her eyes as blue-green

as the sea,

just like mine.

Then I invent an imaginary village

in Spain, for my birthplace,

and I give my age

as twenty,

and I show off

my muscles,

pretending to feel

brave . . .

By the time I board

a dragon-smoky

Panamá Craze steamship,

I've already told so many lies

that my conscience feels

as hollow

as my belly.

MATEO

THE VOYAGE FROM CUBA

Hunger at sea for three days

feels like a knife in the flesh—

twisted blade, rusty metal,

the piercing tip of a long

sharp-edged

dagger

called *regret*.

But there's no turning back,

and with no food on board,

hunger haunts me

until we finally reach

the slick, wet Panamá docks,

where dozens of other ships

are all unloading their fuming,

angry,

hungry

human cargo

in thunderous rain.

MATEO

ARRIVAL IN A STRANGE LAND

As soon as my feet touch the docks,
I rush toward a pile of burlap sacks . . .

The bags are filled with island sugar,
soggy from rain, but it's food, so I rip
the cloth and plunge my sweaty hand
into the sweetness
of my homeland,
wondering
if I will ever
see the island
again.

MATEO

COLOR-CODED

A foreman commands us to line up
by country:

Americans, Frenchmen, Dutch.

Spaniards, Greeks, Italians.

Jamaicans, Barbadians, Haitians.

Each work crew is a different shade
of light or dark,
but when the foreman orders us
to stand still while we're measured
for our coffins,
dark and light faces
all look equally
shocked.

MATEO

THE LABOR TRAIN

Jungle heat sends foggy steam rising

from my hair, like a thick mist

on the towering forest

that looms ahead of the train,

as we crowd onto a flatcar

with open sides.

In order to keep from falling out,

I cling to any surface I can find,

even when

it means leaning

toward the jungle,

grasping at branches.

Behind us, a cattle car enclosed

by a wooden framework

is filled with Jamaicans

and Barbadians, dark islanders

who have to ride behind bars,

as if trapped in a cage.

Jamaica is one of Cuba's

closest neighbors,

but this is the first time

I have ever seen anyone

from another Caribbean island.

Until now, we have always

been separated

by the sea.

How will we work together,

when Jamaicans speak English

and we know only

español?

MATEO

HOWLERS

Ferocious jungle heat
closes in around us, like the blaze
of a glowing oven.

The train steams through deep
forest shade, beneath spidery,
brilliant red flowers
that dangle
from sky-high branches,
like flames.

Some of the rain-shiny leaves
are shaped like green hands,
others like hearts, livers, or kidneys,
making the whole forest seem
like one enormous,
magical creature
with an endless body
and a fiery mind.

Through the chug

and churn

of the train,

I hear clacking cries

from black toucans

with huge rainbow beaks

and eerie howls

from big, hairy monkeys

with shaggy faces that almost look

human . . .

faces with voices

so challenging

that every man on the train

starts howling too.

MATEO

BOXCAR BARRACKS

Exhausted and excited, I jump off
before the train even stops.
There's nothing but mud and jungle
in every direction.

Each step feels as if the hungry earth
is trying to suck my bare feet into
its wet belly.

A sunburned *americano* foreman
separates us into groups of twelve men.

Each group is led to another train car,
this one completely motionless.

Inside, we find twelve cots
draped with lacy mosquito nets,
and twelve blue shirts,

twelve khaki trousers,

twelve pairs of work boots . . .

Some of the men grumble

and curse, but others laugh,

impressed by our own foolishness.

Did we really believe that we would live

in nice houses like the ones we saw

in that tricky recruiter's

pretty pictures

of dining rooms

with tablecloths

and tables?

Our first meal is served outdoors.

Mushy potatoes, stringy meat, soft bread.

But it's food, and it's filling.

None of the Spanish men seem to mind

my rapid Cuban accent as I echo Mami's

old saying about full bellies

and happy hearts.

MATEO

A DIFFERENT HUNGER

Homesickness?
How can I miss the place
I was so desperate to leave?

All night, I lie awake, frightened
by jungle noises. By dawn,
all I want to do
is keep listening
to screeching birds
and howling monkeys—
any wild animal music
to help me escape
from my own scary
human story
of loss.

MATEO

LA YERBERA

While we sit on the train tracks

eating our breakfast of soggy bread

and weak coffee,

a local *yerbera* — an herb girl —

walks toward us with a basket

of leaves, flowers, roots, and twigs

gracefully balanced

on her head.

Some of the men call out to her

with rude kissing noises, so she clasps

the handle of her machete in one hand

and spins the big cane-chopping knife

like a warning as she sings her wares,

chanting about the sharp teeth

of strong garlic to ward away

bloodsucking

vampire bats.

She sings about fragrant

orange blossoms to heal

the wounds of homesickness.

If I had any money, I would buy

her whole mysterious basket

of scented

cures.

ANITA from the Land of Many Butterflies

VOICES

I listen to the lonely boy's tale of a mother lost

and a father damaged, and then I tell him

how I was abandoned in the forest as a baby

and how I was cared for

by an old Cuban healer

who adopted me as her own

granddaughter.

Now, when monkeys howl, frogs sing,

and wings flap, I think of my forest's

natural music

as a serenade

by my own

animal sisters

and animal brothers.

I belong to the trees, and the mud,

and the whispering wind . . .

THE FOREST

1906

THE HOWLER MONKEYS

PEERING DOWN FROM TREES

PIERCING TRAIN SCREAMS

NOISY STRANGERS

CLOSE

CLOSER

TOO CLOSE

STAY AWAY

AWAY FROM OUR TREES

OURS

OURS

OURS

GO

GO

GO

GO

GO

GO

THE GLASS FROGS

PEERING UP FROM MUD

you can't see us

not like those golden frogs

flashing their beauty

because we're not here

pretend we're not here

you can't eat us

we'd taste like clear air

we're transparent

invisible

until night when stars pass through us

moonlight flows into us

we start to sing

we need to sing

we love to sing

sing

sing

sing

A BLUE MORPHO BUTTERFLY

FLOATING OVER THE WORLD

High enough
just high enough

above
all danger

except the sharp beaks
of birds

but high enough
just high enough

to fool the eyes of hungry beings
with our blue wings

just a passing
shimmer
of sky.

THE TREES

ROOTED

Only our branches
Can move

So we dance

With our green
While our roots
Are unseen

And all the legs
And wings
And eyes
Of the world

Forget that we
Are here

Always here
Always.

THE SERPENT CUT
1906

MATEO

THE WORK CREW

Six hundred Spaniards—all hired in Cuba—
now sleep in boxcars. My team of twelve
is a muttering nest of secret plots.

As I listen to the gruff voices
of my angry crew, I barely
understand their raging way
of seeing the world.

Anarchy is their favorite word.
It means no government, no rules.
It means: Cause trouble.
Create chaos.
Dig a deep canal,
and then explode it.
Destroy our own work,
just to defeat the rich men
who pay us.

The anarchists decide to include me,

even though I am so much younger,

and an islander,

and frightened.

So I nod, pretending that I'm willing

to carry their smuggled messages

and smuggled weapons,

but the truth is, I've already lived

in a house of trouble

for too long.

Dodging the fists of an angry

war veteran

was enough to make me

permanently cautious.

MATEO

BACKBREAKING

Nights of imagining anarchy

are terrifying, but days

of lifting and moving

heavy train tracks

are so exhausting

and painful

that I feel

as though I'm being

swallowed

and chewed

by a monster

made of living

breathing

hungry

mud.

Each morning after breakfast,

a labor train steams us down, down, down,

into the depths of an excavation pit

called *Culebra*— "the Serpent."

My doom.

We line up beside a muddy train track

that we are expected to shift

deeper and deeper and deeper

as the Serpent Cut grows

more hellish,

with gigantic mounds of dynamited rock

and swampy dirt

that the spoil trains haul up, up, up,

in endless, dreary, soul-drowning

rain, rain, thunderous, lightning-strike

rain.

To move a track, we have to bend, lift,

heave, and grunt as one,

all of us bursting

with furious curses, screaming

across this impossibly steep

canyon

that we are creating

by moving these tracks

farther and farther downhill,

so that more and more

rock and mud

can be hauled

up and out,

as if we are

struggling

to reach

the fiery

earth's

melted

heart.

HENRY from the island of Jamaica

THE LIFE OF A DIGGER

Jamaican digging crews have to sleep
eighty men to a room, in huge warehouses
like the ones where big wooden crates
of dynamite are stored.

My hands feel like scorpion claws,
clamped on to a hard hard shovel all day,
then curled into fists at night.

At dawn, the steaming labor trains
deliver us by the thousands, down into
that snake pit where we dig
until my muscles feel
as weak as water
and my backbone
is like shattered glass.

But only half the day
is over.

At lunchtime, we see sunburned

American engineers and foremen

eating at tables, in shady tents

with the flaps left open,

so that we have to watch

how they sit on nice chairs,

looking restful.

We also watch the medium-dark

Spanish men, relaxing as they sit

on their train tracks, grinning

as if they know secrets.

We have no place to sit. Not even

a stool. So we stand, plates in hand,

uncomfortable

and undignified.

Back home, I used to dream of saving

enough Panama money

to buy a bit of good farmland

for Momma and my little brothers

and sisters, so that we would all

have plenty to eat.

Now all I want is a chair.

And food with some spice.

And fair treatment.

Justice.

MATEO

TRAPPED

The life of a train-track mover
is grueling. Exhausting. Painful. Dull.
Even worse, the anarchists expect me
to risk my life smuggling their
handwritten newsletters
from one boxcar barracks to another.

So I sneak away at night, planning
to find my way back to the docks,
hoping to board any ship
headed home . . .

but I'm caught by a policeman
and dragged back to my boxcar,
where all of us are warned
that it's too late for escape.

We signed contracts. If we break them,
we'll be arrested and chained.

MATEO

PAYDAY

The payroll office is just a train car

with two windows and two signs:

GOLD. SILVER. My first two

English words.

Our whole crew waits in a slow, snaking

line that leads to the SILVER sign,

while beside us at the GOLD window,

a short, swiftly moving row of *americano*

foremen and steam-shovel drivers

hold out big, floppy cowboy hats

to catch a shower

of gold.

Gold. Just like the bell-bright coins

in that recruiter's magic show

of metallic

music.

When my turn finally comes,

I hold out a cupped palm

to receive a moon-glossy

trickle

of silver.

My pay amounts to a mere

twenty cents per hour

of spirit-crushing

misery.

HENRY

HALF PAY

When the Spanish track-moving crew

goes ahead of us, we watch, we count.

Then our turn comes, and we hold out

eager hands, palms cupped to receive

ten cents per hour.

We've been in Panama only a few days,

and already we're twice as poor

as the Spaniards.

It's just like the sugar fields at home,

where Englishmen own the land

and medium-dark foremen supervise,

while men like me

have to chop, chop, chop,

with sharp machetes that make us

feel like slaves. Waiting to fight.

Ready to escape.

JOHN STEVENS

from the United States of America

Chief Engineer, Panama Canal

TEAMWORK

If I could hire only white Americans,
I would, but they don't want shovel jobs
and they won't work for silver.

Dark islanders are my only choice,
along with a few hundred semi-whites,
just to show the Jamaicans how easily
they can be replaced.

But islanders are childlike, easily bored . . .
so I'm creating a sporting atmosphere
to motivate hard work. I've divided
all the laborers
into ethnic teams.

Hearty competition will spur men
from each nation

to dig faster and shovel

more mud, loading

more and more dirt and rocks

into the

spoil trains.

Maybe I'll even keep score

and publish the names of winners

in newspapers all over the world.

Imagine how proud those Jamaicans

will feel, if they can manage to beat

the French speakers from little islands

like Guadeloupe

and Martinique.

It will probably be

just a matter of time

until islanders start

placing bets.

MATEO

SILVER TOWN

Rain, rain, rain, mud, mud, mud,
and labor so brutally grueling,
and hope draining, and muscle
straining, and filth heaving,
that it's almost impossible for me
to believe that this much muddy sludge
can be moved by ordinary men
instead of giants.

The only relief is payday, no matter
how stingy.

We take our wages to a makeshift town
made of mud
and rum.

In ramshackle tents and market stalls,
vendors from all over the world
shout in a hundred languages.

There are Sikhs from India wearing

colorful turbans, and Chinese doctors

offering strange cures, and Italians selling boots,

Greeks with jars of olives,

Romanians telling fortunes,

indios from Ecuador weaving

fine white hats from dry reeds,

and local children from right here

in Panamá offering lottery tickets

and spicy snacks—corn fritters,

sweet cakes, and fried fish

from the river,

round eyes staring

from greasy heads.

Bullfights.

Cockfights.

Card games.

Dancing girls.

There are so many choices

for ways to spend payday

that I almost feel tempted

to go off by myself and keep my

stingy silver wages so that I can buy

paper and pencils to sketch

every wonder that I see when I walk

through the forest, or even right here,

on this bustling Bottle Alley street

made of mud

and rum.

Long ago, when Mami was alive

and Papi was sane, I had the chance to go

to school for two whole years. I fell in love

with art class, even though I was supposed to

like reading and writing or learning math

and geography.

I never imagined that I would work

in one of the faraway places I studied

on those big, flat maps that made me

long to paint the whole world

with bright colors.

Now, while most of the Spanish men

rush off to bullfights and others vanish

into tents where I imagine that secret

anarchist meetings

must be going on, I roam alone,

wondering what to do with the rest

of my life.

Each saloon has separate entrances

for silver men and gold, so I slip in

through a silver door, but not too far,

just barely inside—until slowly, I end up

edging closer and closer

to a boxing ring

where a young Jamaican

is fighting a young Barbadian,

both of them wearing the names

of their islands on scribbled signs

that dangle around their necks.

The sight of fists should send me

scurrying for safety, but so far away

from my drunken father, I begin

to wonder how it would feel

to fight back.

When the Barbadian loses,

the Jamaican goes up against

a Trinidadian, and when the new man

is knocked out, I leap forward,

and without any sign to name

my island, I flail

wild punches

and kicks,

imagining

that my enemy

is Papi.

HENRY

THE BOXING MATCH

I could say it's the rum,

but it's really those humiliating

lunches, watching Spaniards

lounging on train tracks

while I have to eat

standing up

like an animal

in a corral.

Each punch I throw

at this inexperienced kid

feels like a bite

of strong strong spice,

making all those

shameful mealtimes

a little more

tasty.

MATEO

AFTER THE FIGHT

Losing is so familiar that I almost feel
as though I'm home.

I walk out of the saloon alone, slogging
across Bottle Alley, this street of muddy
lost dreams.

Like a vision from the forest, *la yerbera*
appears—Anita, the herb girl—with her
delicately balanced
enormous basket
of twigs and petals
that seem to overflow
like a magical fountain
as she sings:
willow bark for pain,
basil stems for peace of mind,
goosefoot *epazote* leaves
to charm the gas out of beans . . .

She looks like a ruffled forest bird,

with her colorful skirts and a necklace

of green feathers strung between red seeds

and the blue wings of huge

shimmering

butterflies.

Without any way to paint her true beauty,

I pull one of the twigs from her basket

and scratch a rough shadow

of her smile

in mud.

ANITA

RARE CURES

Mateo asks the price of *azafrán*—
saffron, the most expensive spice
because it is the golden pollen
of a tiny purple crocus flower,
gathered one strand at a time
by my own hand.

Mateo's fists are bruised, his cheeks
blood-streaked. Has he been arguing
in the dance halls, fighting over a girl?
The thought makes my basket feel
as protective as a helmet.

But he looks too sad for real wildness,
so I give him a bit of the fragrant spice
as a gift, to help him remember
his mother's kitchen
and to thank him

for the strange

little portrait, pressed

into mud.

Then I leave him standing

as if dazed, while I roam away

from Silver Town, back into

my forest,

my musical

green home.

THE FOREST

1906

THE HOWLER MONKEYS

DYNAMITE

WE HATE YOUR BOOM

WE FEAR YOUR BLAST

WE ROAR OUR FURY

OUR RAGE

OUR TERROR

OUR HORROR

OF STRANGERS

WITH EXPLOSIONS

SO MUCH LOUDER

THAN OUR OWN

POWERFUL

POWERFUL

POWERFUL

VOICES

AS WE HOWL

GO AWAY GO AWAY GO AWAY

GO GO GO GO GO GO GO GO GO

A MONKEY-EATING EAGLE

PEERING DOWN FROM SKY

Smaller monkeys are tasty

but big hairy howlers

are the meatiest

so I search from high above

for dark specks in treetops

far below

so far

yet easy enough to pierce

with sharp talons

after I plummet

down

from

hunger

to

my wild

forest feast.

A THREE-TOED SLOTH

PEERING UP FROM A BRANCH

Above me, a loud monkey vanishes,
but I'm slow and silent;
no eagle can see me
dangling
upside down
with green plants growing
all over my shaggy hair.

Beetles munch my algae.
Moths nest on my shoulders.
No one knows that I'm an animal
instead of a tree limb.

Time
is my friend:
I can wait for weeks
just to move; I can eat so slowly,
just one delicious leaf
at a time.

A TREE VIPER

GREEN SNAKE OR GREEN PLANT?

j
u
s
t
a
v
i
n
e
u
n
t
i
l
I

BITE

THE TREES

SHRINKING

It never seemed as if anything

could make our huge trunks

smaller

but men

with machines and explosives

have made some of us

vanish

leaving the others

lonely

for

time

more time

sun, soil, growth,

while some of us shrink, others survive

and grow, grow, grow . . .

THE COCKROACH SLIDE

1906

MATEO

NOSTALGIA

With no way to cook my own food,

I add a single precious strand

of the herb girl's golden saffron

to my dreary

Serpent Cut lunch

of plain white rice.

The aroma helps me remember

the best part of my past,

when Mami was still alive

and Papi knew the difference

between wartime

and family life.

Each whiff of scented spice

smells like a memory

of happiness.

MATEO

SLEEP

After another agonizing day of bending

to lift ponderous train tracks,

my back feels as twisted

as a tangled vine in the jungle.

Spine-shredding

arm-wrenching

spirit-crushing

labor

makes me wish

for any job that would feel

like an accomplishment

instead of torture.

In the evening, I listen to howlers

and I dream of Anita, creating

a night world that makes me

smile.

Later, nightmares send my hands

thrashing through the mosquito net

that hangs above my cot . . .

Biting insects get in through the holes,

leaving me itchy and bleeding

and sad.

HENRY

SLEEPLESS

Troubled by wishes, I get up

and step outside, where I listen

to rain, rain, gruesome rain,

the night sky as thick

and slick as a waterfall,

the drumming of thunder

so furious that it makes

sleepless monkeys

howl . . .

Long after the noisy noisy downpour

is over, I can still hear raindrops slipping

down from one layer of leaves to another,

until finally they settle beside my feet

in swampy mud,

where singing frogs hop

and squirming leeches cling

to my ankles.

If only I could find some way

to take a steamship home

and start my life over.

I've never had a chance

to go to school. If I send enough

silver home, will my little brothers

and sisters be able to study?

Maybe one of them will even

grow up to be

a teacher

or a nurse.

That would make all my Serpent Cut

suffering

worthwhile.

MATEO

DAYDREAMS

Bend.

Lift.

Heave.

Grunt.

Ache.

Howl!

Escape from the pain

by imagining

the friendly herb girl

with her necklace

of feathers

and wings . . .

HENRY

HATRED

I'm so sick of rain, mud, shovels,

and that SILVER payroll window!

I hate seeing the bloodied face

of the loser boy at payday fights.

Why does he keep trying to beat me?

He never wins any share of the bets.

Can it be that maybe he's exactly

like me, just feeling a little bit crazy

from all this bitter bitter

Panama Craze

disappointment?

MATEO

POSSIBILITIES

On fight nights, I always meet Anita,
and while we visit, she gives me a balm
of wild herbs for my bruises.

She tries to talk me out of violence,
but when I point out her machete,
she insists it's her only protection
against poisonous snakes
and mean men.

I can't imagine being brave
if I were a girl, alone in the forest . . .

but when I tell Anita my thoughts,
she laughs and says girls are just
like boys—all they want
is fairness
and respect.

ANITA

MAYBE

I know I'm too young to really flirt,
but sometimes I do enjoy talking
to the *cubano* boy
instead of working . . .

and sometimes, on Sundays, I love
hearing the Jamaicans who sing
in makeshift Silver Town churches,
instead of listening
only to birds, frogs, monkeys,
and dreams . . .

so maybe I won't always stay
quite so far away from human
possibilities.

MATEO

CAUTION

On free Sundays, some men doze,

while others pray, or drink, or moan

about the heat, rain, mosquitoes, biting ants,

stinging wasps, ticks, tarantulas, scorpions,

snakes, sore muscles, bone aches,

brain boredom,

and loneliness.

In an effort to get away from anarchists

who expect me to carry their newsletters

all over the jungle, I roam alone

like a wild creature, stashing

the pamphlets in hollow logs

and old tractors

instead of delivering them

to dangerous strangers.

ANITA

A MYSTERY

I follow Mateo, without letting him
see me.

I know how to hide. I've been sneaky
all my life. It's the only way to survive
in a land of hunters
and hunted.

I watch as he tucks a stack of papers into
the rusty metal husks of huge machines
abandoned by France many years ago,
after that nation tried and failed to dig
all the way across
my forest.

I try to imagine Mateo's island.
Are there sights that he treasures
the same way I love and need

the wild height

of these trees?

I have seen so many skillful little sketches

that Mateo makes in mud with a stick.

There are people, animals, birds,

and nameless shapes that could be

winged spirits—sometimes it's not easy

to tell the difference when you live

in a place of transformations, where

caterpillars emerge as butterflies,

tadpoles change into frogs,

and tiny seeds grow

until they reach

the comforting size

of whispery

forest giants.

When Mateo is gone, I creep

toward the tractors and peek

at the hidden papers, expecting

drawings or paintings or a diary,

but all I find is mysterious writing

in a language I can't

understand.

HENRY

FREEDOM

Other diggers tell me that if I ever see
a gold-colored frog, I should catch it
and care for it, until the frog rewards me
by turning into real gold.

So one morning I reach down and pull
a black-speckled, bright yellow frog
out of the mud. I can feel its tiny heart
pulsing
in my hand.

Then I let it go, hoping that if the legend
is true and golden frogs really can
turn into valuable valuable jewels,
then maybe I'll find this one again
someday, when it's made out of metal,
and I won't feel like a warden
guarding a captive.

MATEO

FEVERISH

A fury of blazing sun turns to sweat.
A chill in the evening follows. I lie awake
in my soggy clothes, wishing for a blanket
or a clean shirt, any small source
of comfort . . .

Shivering, I listen to the music of tree frogs,
crickets, night monkeys, and screech owls,
a whole orchestra of predators
and prey.

Why don't all those singing animals
fall silent? Can't they hear that hidden
jaguar's silence?

This fever feels like a hungry beast too.
How long will its flame fangs take
to devour me?

ANITA

FLOODS

At the height of the rainy season,

forest trails turn into swamps,

so I row from village to village

in an old dugout canoe

so moist that mosses and ferns

sprout from cracks

in the splintered wood.

I can't let something as common as water

keep me from working to help sick people

by brewing teas and potions from herbs

that I must keep finding and gathering

right here in my vast garden, this forest,

my world of pain

and cures . . .

As I glide past huts propped on stilts,

children smile and wave

from beneath big leaves

that their mothers call

"poor man's umbrellas."

When the furious rain pounds down

so hard and fast that my little canoe

starts to fill up with water,

I try to scoop it out

with a coconut shell,

but the flow is too swift,

so I have to give up

and drift back toward my home,

a jungle inn called La Cubana María,

after my adoptive grandma, an old

island herb woman

who has cared for me

since I was tiny.

She is the one who still teaches me

how to heal every strange

human sorrow

except

my own.

Is it foolish for me to wish

that someday I might meet

my true mother?

OLD MARIA from the island of Cuba

MY CLINIC-INN

I was here long before the Americans,
before the French, even before the bold
adventurers from many lands who flocked
across Panamá back when it still belonged
to Colombia, and greedy crowds
from every nation on earth
were making their way
to the California gold rush.

There were no doctors in this forest,
so when a traveler fell ill, he came here,
seeking cures from the power of plants.

By the time an abandoned baby was found
in one of the rooms, I was old and tired,
but caring for little Anita gave me energy,
so I held her, and fed her, and taught her
the art of offering
hope.

ANITA

DANGER

There is nothing I love more
than listening to *la vieja* María
tell tales
of long ago.

If I survived without a mother, then
maybe others will survive now, when
each day brings news of death.

As the Serpent Cut grows deeper,
rain softens the mud and landslides
swallow laborers. Wheels of vultures
circle high above the pit, eager to fill
their winged hunger.

I try to talk Mateo into running away
from his contract, but his fear of policemen
is greater than his fear
of landslides.

MATEO

SLIDING

When my crew is assigned to a slope
called *la Cucaracha*— "the Cockroach" —
we all feel doomed.
Dynamite blasts send
giant hissing insects into the air
around our heads,
while pit viper snakes
slither close to our boots.

Each explosion is more risky than the last.
Layers of mud between layers of stone
are shoveled into dirt trains by Jamaicans,
while we bend,
heave,
lift,
groan,
pray,
and slip
down, down, down,

shoved

by a mudslide,

pushed

toward death.

HENRY

BURIED

Mud all around me

beneath and above

mud that boils

roars

and rumbles

crushes my breath

steals my voice

mud that covers

the future

and buries me

in gloom.

MATEO

DESPERATE

Every survivor leaps to help,

all of us digging side by side,

silver and gold men

equally grateful

to be alive!

Our digging is urgent

but careful,

just in case any buried men

might be injured by our frantic,

trembling, pounding

shovels.

HENRY

RESCUED

Face

to

face

only a thin sheet of mud

between us

hands

reach for my arms

as my

voice returns

to thank the loser boy

who is right here

so close

his familiar eyes suddenly

the eyes

of a friend.

MATEO

ARRESTED

After the landslide, somehow I expect

a few days off—a chance to feel relieved

that I survived and grateful that I helped

rescue the Jamaican boxer—

but this *Cucaracha* slope

never gives me a rest.

I have to keep working, and wishing,

and even though I haven't hidden

any anarchist pamphlets lately,

one night, during a lightning storm,

police break into the boxcar and awaken us

with clubs, beating us, then dragging us

away to prison.

MATEO

QUESTIONED

During days as dark as night,

I'm chained in a windowless cell.

No light.

No air.

Just questions.

And fists.

During days as lonely as nights,

I grow more anxious

for answers.

ANITA

KICKERS

The prison is called *Renacer*— "Rebirth" —
because men who go in big and strong
are said to come out as weak
and helpless
as babies.

But Mateo's arrest is absurd.
He's accused of being a kicker journalist,
one of the rebellious writers of articles
about the canal's engineering troubles
and labor troubles, landslides, fevers,
failures, protests.

I know for a fact that Mateo did not write
those pamphlets.
I saw the words in *Gallego, Catalán*.
Languages from Spain.
Regional dialects that no islander knows.

So I take all my money

to the police, and I pay a hefty bribe,

adding a few threats just to terrify

the officers, who fear the secret magic

of women with poisonous

native herbs.

MATEO

RELEASED

I don't know why the police let me go,

but once I'm back in the boxcar,

I see that three men

are still missing,

while the others fume with rage,

whispering about the real reason

for our arrest

and interrogation—

preparation for an official visit

from the president

of the United States.

THEODORE ROOSEVELT

from the United States of America

President and Commander in Chief

MAKING DIRT FLY

No president has ever left American soil
while in office, but Chief Engineer Stevens
complains that the morale of laborers
is at an all-time low, so I've decided
to visit the Serpent Cut.

This trip will make history.
Tourists from all over the world
are already perched on the rim
of the pit, peering down
with opera glasses, as I pose
at the controls of a ninety-five-ton
Bucyrus steam shovel, a machine
so massive that newspaper photos
will inspire confidence in America's
power.

All around me, workers with shovels

are making the mud fly, the white

Americans supervising while black

islanders dig, on hillsides

so steep

and unstable

that it would be a real

waste to risk wrecking

valuable

machines.

HENRY

THE VIEW FROM BELOW

All those fancy fancy tourists

way up there on the rim of the pit

must be staring down at us

and thinking

that we look

as tiny

as rows

and rows

of scurrying

ants.

The American president

on his smoky steam shovel

must look like a knight

riding a dragon.

ANITA

UNNATURAL

Roosevelt's visit brings tourists rushing

into my forest, searching for adventure,

but they don't buy herbs; all they want

is hats—white hats like the American president's,

hats woven in Ecuador, hats that tourists

insist on calling Panamá hats. Don't they

understand that Latin America

has many countries?

Tourist ladies want dead birds fastened

to their hats—whole birds, not just a few

stray feathers dropped by living birds,

like the ones I wear on my necklace.

Tourist ladies walk around with orioles

on their hats, hummingbirds, egrets,

even owls. Can't they feel the ghostly

bird eyes staring down

from the tops of their heads?

The tourists ask for whole collections
of rare butterflies for their children—
wild butterflies, caught and pinned,
not just a few drifting wings,
like the ones I find after migrations.

And they want skins. Jaguar. Puma. Snake.
And crocodile teeth, peccary tusks,
fossil shark teeth from the Serpent Cut.
Anything sharp, so they can pretend
they know danger.

Monkey hands are the most popular
souvenir. All over Silver Town, vendors
get rich by hunting, then chopping off,
the hairy fingers.

When I gaze up at the trees, I see
the frightened howlers and I hear
the fading songs of doomed birds.

THE FOREST

1906

THE HOWLER MONKEYS

HUNTERS

WE DREAD

STENCH

NOISE

SMOKE

GUNS

WE HURL OUR WASTE

DOWN

BUT HUNTERS

DON'T FLEE

SO WE LEAP

TO A NEW TREE

WE GO

GO

GO

GO

THE GIANT HISSING COCKROACHES

SURPRISE

we dart

    hiss

fly

    we startle
any snake
    that tries
to eat
    our giant
wings

THE CROCODILES

PATIENCE

We wait

All day

All night

Resting

Between

Mossy

Logs

Always

Ready

For

Any

Passing

Canoe

Or

Thirsty

Tourist.

A JAGUAR

A TRUE HUNTER'S SILENCE

THE TREES

SHATTERED

When a steam shovel rolls

over

our roots

we sigh

but only the wind

and rain

seem to hear

as we slow

our growth

of twigs

and leaves

while we struggle to repair

our roots

our roots.

CURIOSITY

1906

MATEO

DRY SEASON

Heat rages and dust slides,
leaving spidery cracks
in the hard
red soil.

Towering trees are chopped down
to build more and more railroad tracks,
more gold houses, silver barracks,
and fancy hotels, so that tourists
can stare down in elegant safety
from the high, sturdy rim
of our danger. As they watch
our dusty muscles, can they see
our weary dreams?

Impossible. Impossible. Impossible.
How can such a monstrous ditch
ever be finished?

HENRY

TRANSLATION

We give up the payday fights. We feel
like brothers.
Mateo teaches me Spanish,
and I guide him through English,
and together, we start to feel
as if we just don't know anything.

Each *palabra* of *español* is so flowery
and roundabout. Why can't words
simply sound like their meanings, like
"blunt blunt" and "clear clear"?

A few weeks ago, I never would have
imagined that Mateo and I could share
any hopes or wishes,
but landslides
and languages
change everything.

Now all we crave

is victory

in our shared

struggle

to understand

anything.

MATEO

WORDLESS

English is impossible. Nothing is predictable.
One vowel can turn into a thousand and one
different sounds.

On workdays, Henry and I have to talk
with our hands, waving signals across
the dry-season dust.

He is always far below, digging dirt
to load the spoil trains that can only haul
their ponderous burden uphill
after we've finished our slow task
of moving these railroad tracks
down,
down,
down toward the Jamaican crew's
eerie zone
of unimaginable
danger.

AUGUSTO from the island of Puerto Rico

SCIENCE

Understanding tricky soil has turned me

into a desperate man,

constantly anxious,

eager to save lives

like the lives of those two funny boys

who wave strong arms

the way golden frogs wave tiny legs—

sending signals across all barriers

of distance, language,

and segregation.

One misplaced dynamite blast

and this whole dusty *Cucaracha* slide

will roll like new snow

off a slanted

upstate New York roof.

When I moved to the U.S. mainland,

it was meant to be for just a few years,

but I stayed on in New York to study

for a doctorate in geology, learning

fragments of other natural sciences

along the way. Those Panama Craze

recruiters really knew what they were doing

when they convinced me

that simply because my island homeland

is a possession of the United States,

I can be paid in gold, like a white

American,

instead of silver,

like other islanders

from independent nations.

Now I have plenty of money, but all I feel

is shame

for the segregation

and fear

for all the laborers

my maps

are expected to protect.

How can I predict landslides?

Mud and dust aren't the same as rock,

with its solid crystals and rigid

behavior.

Mud and dust love to mix, churn, and roll,

like flooded rivers or human

thoughts.

Mud and dust almost have

personalities. They seem to be alive.

Like scoundrels. True villains.

Enemies.

MATEO

THE MAP MAN

At lunchtime, a *puertorriqueño* sketches
with his charcoal pencil while I peer
over his shoulder, wondering why
he chooses to sit on our
hard, hot train tracks
when he could be resting
in a shady dining tent,
enjoying gold food
and cool comfort.

When I ask, he admits that he misses
mixing languages. Then he rapidly
switches back and forth between
English *y español* as he shows me how
to sketch birds in flight—dazzling flocks
of green parrots, scarlet macaws,
rainbow toucans, yellow orioles,
and purple-throated fruitcrows,

all passing high above us, as if
culebras y cucarachas—serpents
and cockroaches—did not exist.

Augusto draws portraits of me up close
and of Henry off in the distance, waving,
and he sketches the coiled snakes,
giant roaches, and fluttering clouds
of colorful butterflies as they land
on dry dust, tasting the red earth
as they search
for nutritious salts.

Augusto writes an English name
on each butterfly portrait:
clearwing, swordtail, daggerwing,
swallowtail, owl.

He explains that this last kind
has huge owl-eye designs
on its wide brown wings,

fake eyes for tricking hungry jays

into thinking that they are the ones

in danger

of getting gobbled.

I am fascinated by the way

this map man

mixes two languages

and the way he mixes

science

and art.

When a coatimundi scurries

onto the train tracks, begging for crumbs

from our lunches, Augusto quickly sketches

the lively animal's pointy face

and long, jaunty tail. Coatis are cute,

but I keep my distance. Sharp teeth

are perilous. Augusto calls them

ice picks. Since I've never touched ice,

I have to guess how the coldness

of frozen water might feel . . .

Henry should see this, I tell myself
as I study the clever map man's expert
artwork.

But as usual, Henry is far below,
shoveling and suffering, ankle-deep
in red dust, then motionless as he gazes
up at us while he eats his angry,
no-place-to-sit, mushy lunch.

So, in order to tell him about it later,
I memorize these new English words
I've learned today: *Daggerwing.*
Ice pick. Artwork.

Artwork, because until I saw Augusto's
confident way of sketching, I did not realize
that my uncertain, timid way
is not art. All I've ever accomplished
with my tensely held, self-conscious pencil
is a stiff imitation of rigid objects,
not this free-spirited, midair magic.

AUGUSTO

AN ASSISTANT

I've needed help for a long time,
someone to carry my art supplies
on Sunday expeditions, and dust off
all the books in my house, and organize
bones, feathers, statues, and seashells
in my curiosity cabinets.

But we're allowed to hire
silver servants only if they have special
permission to work in the gold zone.
So I help Mateo obtain papers. He's listed
as a Spaniard, even though his voice
sounds so Caribbean.

He seems eager to earn a bit of extra cash
on free Sundays, and I plan to help him
develop his natural skill. He sketches
like a child, but his talent
is enormous.

MATEO

BEYOND FENCES

Until now, I've seen gold houses only

from a distance, along the edges

of separate gold American towns

where policemen on horseback

chase silver men away

if we try to watch

gold ball games

or gather bananas

and mangoes

from gold gardens.

As Augusto's new helper, I can walk

right into his fancy clubhouse, where

gold men sit reading under ceiling fans

that spin like enchanted dragonflies,

cooling the afternoon air.

The houses of married gold men

are huge, but even the small rooms

reserved for bachelors like Augusto

feel spacious and peaceful

compared to crowded boxcars.

Dusting all the strange marvels

in the map man's curiosity cabinets

helps me feel like an adventurer

instead of a servant. Horns. Tusks.

Sun-bleached bones. Stone figurines

of birds and frogs, carved by tribesmen

who lived on the Serpent Cut

just a few years ago,

when it was still a forested

mountain.

How swiftly things change—a few short

days ago, I could never have guessed

that I would ever be willing to give up

even one treasured minute with Anita,

but now, on Sundays when Augusto

takes me exploring

out in the wilderness,

I feel certain

that I was born to

learn.

Maybe the map man will let Anita

come with us. She could help him

find rare treasures

that only a local

would know.

AUGUSTO

THE MUSEUM OF MEMORY

Young Mateo's fascination
with expeditions
and curiosity cabinets
reminds me how I marveled
when my father took me camping
or onto a university campus to visit
his Time Lab, in the museum
where he studied the skeletons
of extinct giant lizards, woolly
mammoths, and saber-toothed tigers
that seemed so alive.

There was a Spirit Lab too,
with pickled creatures floating
in green glass jars, like liquid
ghosts,
and a mysterious building
that Papa called the Maze
of Lost Scientists,

where specialists peered

into microscopes, each one working

year after year until he knew more

than anyone else on earth

about a particular species

of orchid, spider, centipede,

or worm. The specialists

were jokingly nicknamed

Flower Man, Dr. Tarantula,

Lord Centipede, or Mr. Maggot.

By Mateo's age, I was already known

as Bird Boy, a student of feathers

and topography—an odd mapmaking term

adopted by naturalists to describe the study

of bird anatomy, as if wings

might turn out to be landscapes

that invite

exploration.

Geological engineering was my grandpa's

idea, a practical course of study, leading

to steady work. But now, each and every

glorious, hot, sweaty Sunday afternoon,

I am once again Bird Boy, a grown man

kept young and hopeful

by venturing far and wide

to investigate

the unknown.

MATEO

WINGED ART

Augusto shows me how he paints

swift portraits

of wings

in a bright sky,

as flocks of brilliant birds soar

past his window

like dreams . . .

If only I could be free to fly

on paper

all week,

turning each day

into an expedition

of the curious mind

and observant eye.

But Mondays are workdays.

Bend. Heave. Lift. Grunt. Ache.

Sigh.

ANITA

ALMOST INVISIBLE

When Mateo tells me about his Sunday job,
I sneak into the gold zone, the best place
for selling remedies that cure loneliness
to the homesick wives
of American engineers.

I glance up at Augusto's window
and see Mateo painting on canvas,
just like a real artist. Suddenly, life
seems as changeable
as a clearwing butterfly
that appears green when it rests
on a leaf, brown on a twig,
or blue in a cloudless sky.

I imagine I must be changing too,
but when those clear wings are your own,
it's impossible to detect all the hidden
mysterious details.

MATEO

COMPLETELY MAGNIFICENT

Augusto gives me art supplies
and lessons, so that I can paint
every amazing creature I see:
a slow-moving
boa constrictor,
two swiftly sprinting whiptail lizards,
and all the gigantic rodents that graze
on gold-zone lawns—cat-size agoutis
and dog-size capybaras, none of them
afraid to be captured
by my paintbrush.

Anita is thrilled to accompany us
each time we pack up our supplies
and go out exploring for iridescent
hummingbirds and resplendent
green quetzal birds with impossibly
long, shimmering tails that make us
wonder if we are dreaming.

ANITA

MY GARDEN OF CURES

Climbing
heals me.

Treetops
soothe me.

Mysteries like army ants and bullet ants
threaten me.

High in the leafy layers
of my forest mother's canopy,
my body seems as slow and awkward
as a grinning sloth's, but my mind
feels
winged
as I dodge small dangers, listening
to the trees and birds, while far below,
Mateo paints.

THE FOREST

1906

THE HOWLER MONKEYS

FOOD

WE LOVE LEAVES

WE LIKE FRUIT

WE EAT

ALL DAY

WE HOWL

AT SUNSET

WE DREAM

ALL NIGHT

NO MORE NOISE

UNTIL DAWN

THE RUBY-THROATED HUMMINGBIRD

MIGRATION

Returning from north to south

I cross
the wide sea
alone

never resting
above waves waves waves

and then this green land
of winter warmth

my exhaustion complete

until I find
the sweet flowers
this nectar
my life.

THE ARMY ANTS

TOGETHER

we move in droves hordes masses

we line up and march
we eat every creature in our path
living or dead

we strip the meat off all the bones
we eat muscle sinew fat

we march until nothing is left
but our movement

we march march march
falling into water
making bridges
of our bodies

so the rest of us can march march march
and eat eat eat

THE BULLET ANT

SOLITARY

I move through leaves
alone

it takes only
one sting

to keep me safe
from mouths
that eat

and feet
that crush

I live
with fear
and power—
my sting

THE TREES

WILDERNESS

We are fewer
than before,

but each of us
is just as alive
as ever,

our leaves
hungry for sunlight,
our roots thirsty
for rain,

our fruit and seeds carried far
by flying birds and roaming animals
so that young trees can sprout and grow,
our shared forest once again spreading
like music.

THE SILVER WARD

1907

MATEO

ANOTHER YEAR

Seasons of rain, mud, dust,
raging sun,
furious fevers.

This heat of burning muscles
and blazing fears,
the harsh heat
of sheer weariness,
as I slice my way deeper and deeper
into the fiery loss
of time.

I am not old yet, but at fifteen,
I no longer
feel young.

HENRY

CRATE TOWN

So much of the silver I earn
goes right back to the Americans
as payment for my cot in the barracks
and payment for those shameful, no-taste,
stand-up-in-mud,
spiceless meals.

Even though I always manage to send
a bit of silver home to Momma, it's never
enough to feel as though I still belong
to a real real family.

All around me, hundreds of Jamaicans move
out of the barracks, into the jungle,
where they sleep in shacks made from empty
dynamite crates, and buy rice and beans
in Silver Town, and cook over campfires,
just so they can eat sitting down,
feeling human.

MATEO

PRECARIOUS

Augusto calls Henry's crate town
un precario, because the shacks
can be swept away by floods,
or flared away
by cooking flames,
or smashed by policemen
when they rampage, searching
for runaways.

I long to move too—
out of the barracks
and into the wild jungle—but it means
hiking all the way to a labor train
each morning and all the way back
from the train each evening—
hiking, hiking, hiking,
no matter how weary
the feet, no matter how weary
the heart.

So I try it, and soon I discover

that I can never willingly return

to the dangers of sharing

a small, crowded barracks-car

with anarchists.

I prefer the dangers of wilderness.

Crocodiles, serpents, and jaguars

are not nearly as frightening

as angry men.

On Sundays, Henry and I buy food

for the week, so that after work,

we can cook out in the open, adding

as many hot peppers as we want,

along with a sample of Anita's

saffron, ginger, and cinnamon.

Then we sit

together,

medium-dark

and dark-dark,

as if

the bizarre

Canal Zone rules

did not

matter.

They don't.

AUGUSTO

OMINOUS NEWS

Chief Engineer Stevens

has abruptly resigned,

discouraged by rain, mud, fever,

and landslides, and by islanders

who are moving out to the jungle

by the thousands, so that they

show up for work only

half the time.

President Roosevelt has already

appointed a replacement.

The new chief is an Army man

who threatens to run the canal

like a war against

nature.

GEORGE W. GOETHALS

from the United States of America

Chief Engineer, Panama Canal

Chairman, Isthmian Canal Commission

ONE-MAN RULE

Roosevelt insisted that I take this crazy job,

so I made him sign an executive order

that I wrote myself, giving me full control

of every aspect of Canal Zone life:

Labor. Housing. Hospitals. All of it

is mine. I'm the only judge and jury,

and the only Constitution, and because

we're far beyond U.S. borders,

there won't be any need

for a Bill of Rights.

I've already outlawed labor unions

for American steam-shovel drivers,

and if the gold men don't like it,

they can bring their complaints

directly to me. Face to face.

Man to man. No go-betweens.

No negotiations.

I've set a digging quota too.

Three million cubic yards of dirt

each month. Under Stevens, the workers

dug only a fraction of that

in two years.

I'm a military man, so this will be

my personal war against mud.

I expect a complete and absolute

victory.

JACKSON SMITH

from the United States of America

Manager, Department of Labor, Quarters,
and Subsistence

HOUSING

Goethals runs the war against mud,

but I control houses and barracks.

That's why all the workers call me

Square Foot Smith, because I give

every white American gold man

one square foot of housing

for every dollar he's earned

per month on the job.

When reporters ask me

about conditions for silver men,

I explain that the dark races

are ignorant—they prefer to live

in boxcars or out in the jungle, so

there's no point giving them

extra clothes

or dry blankets.

They would just get

everything

dirty.

MATEO

THE BRAIN WAGON

Nights in the makeshift crate town
feel like a crazy escape.

Along with my treasured Sundays,
freedom-crazed living helps me feel
stronger. I love exploring the forest
with Augusto, who teaches me to sketch
birds, frogs, butterflies,
and Anita, smiling
beneath her basket
of magic.

Mondays always feel unreal,
with Goethals patrolling the pit
in a yellow electric train car
that he calls his Brain Wagon.
From its safety, he studies our danger,
then makes his warlike decisions
about mud.

HENRY

MONKEY HILL

The war against mud

belongs to Goethals,

but the wounds

and the losses

are ours.

Layers of rock tumble,

sheets of sludge slide,

and the mule-drawn

death wagon

rolls back and forth,

delivering islanders

to a hilltop graveyard,

where howlers, way up

in the green green trees,

shriek and moan

like lonely

phantoms.

MATEO

THE HOSPITAL

Malaria strikes me
like a fist of flame.
Heat, chills, shivers,
and half-awake
fever dreams.

When I slump down at work,
I'm carried away from the mud
in a mule-drawn ambulance

and then lifted onto a train
that whisks me away
to a sweaty cot
in the silver ward,

where I gulp foul-tasting medicine:
bitter quinine, my only
hope.

ANITA

HEALING

I hover close to Mateo's cot.
Finding him here, so sick and so weak,
is a shock, even though I sell herbs
in this dismally dreary hospital
often enough to see much worse.

The hospital is divided into sections.
Silver men. Gold men. Women.

There is a ward for uncurables too,
desolate yellow-fever patients who are
quarantined behind screens, so that if
a stray mosquito bites one, it can't
get out and bite a healthy
doctor or nurse to pass on
the dreaded disease.

I make sure Mateo doesn't swallow
too much quinine, the brewed bark

of a cinchona tree, the only cure
for malaria. Without the bitter remedy,
his liver and kidneys would fail.
He would die . . .

But too much quinine
can leave a malaria patient
blind, or deaf, or both,
like the helpless beggars
who haunt Bottle Alley.

Mateo doesn't
recognize me.

His fever-melted mind
seems as lost as the heart
of a traveler
who strays
too far
from any
known trail.

MATEO

REALITY?

A nurse with the smile
of the herb girl, but wiser,
a grownup . . .

or is she just one more illusion,
a feverish
wish dream?

If only I could tell
the difference between daylight
and night dreams.

ANITA

PATIENCE

The silver ward is hideous.
Mateo languishes in a gloomy room
that faces a swamp,

while gold men in their clean ward
receive a sea breeze so refreshing
that nurses call it The Doctor.

I stay in the despicable hospital
until I'm certain that Mateo
is regaining his strength
and his clarity
of mind,
even though it means convincing
tough American nurses
to let me break a few silly
gold-silver rules.

MATEO

GOLD NURSES

The white-winged hats of these women

comfort me, and so do their stubborn,

helpful minds. Most of them were hired

on my home island, where they gained

their healing experience

during the war they call Spanish-American,

even though it was really our war

for independence from Spain, a Cuban war

that was seized by the United States

for its own purposes.

Now, with the battles long forgotten,

I listen as gold nurses tell Anita

their bold opinions about voting rights

for women—all women, not just gold ones.

It's the strangest idea I've ever heard,

but after a wild fever, wild ideas

seem to make sense.

ANITA

INDEPENDENCE

Suddenly, I understand why Mateo
was so eager to go off with Augusto,
even when it meant spending less
time with me.

I need time of my own too. Time to listen
to these nurses. Time to ride with them
when they invite me to patrol a bridge
on horseback — a bridge where gold men
throw goats and chickens down
into a river where crocodiles
thrash and writhe, fighting
for flesh, a cruel entertainment
for bored men.

The nurses explain that crocodiles
soon learn to expect food when they see
humans. The ugly sport sends reptiles
swimming upriver, to villages

where they hunt

children.

How often do bored people

dream up strange games

without thinking

of the wild

consequences?

So I ride with the nurses,

and I watch as they shoot rifles

to scare the cruel gold men

away.

GERTRUDE BEEKS

from the United States of America

Welfare Department of the National Civic Federation

REFORMS

When I worked with Jane Addams at Hull-House,
I knew we could improve living conditions
for women, but now President Roosevelt
has asked me to study the difficult daily lives
of sixty-five thousand workers—male and female—
from all over the world. I hardly know
where to start.

But I rally my courage, and with hordes
of reporters in tow, I boldly visit everyone
from stern Goethals
and that horrible
Square Foot Smith
right down to the poorest,
most miserable
islanders.

Wages. Hours. Sanitation. Recreation.
Clothing. Food. Every detail
matters.

I recommend hot showers for American
housing, and drying sheds for American
laundry, and social clubs for American
women, and good schools for American
children. I recommend fumigation crews
to spray mosquito-killing oil on puddles
and ponds in American gardens.
Without spray crews, there's no hope
of controlling deadly malaria
and yellow fever.

But hospitals are my greatest challenge.
Men are separated, but the women's area
is an emotional disaster, with pale ladies
from Boston and Iowa fuming
about having to share a ward
with dark-skinned washerwomen

from the Bahamas

and Martinique.

As soon as Americans arrive in Panama,

even northerners begin to act

like southerners.

But I am not expected to change

this strange system of racial separation.

All I can do for silver people is suggest

to that odious Square Foot Smith

that he give each laborer a blanket

to prevent pneumonia and an extra

shirt so that one can be washed

and dried while the other

is worn.

Lives could be saved

by something as simple

as a few

scraps

of cloth.

But I don't imagine

that Square Foot Smith

will care.

MATEO

AFTER A FEVER

Anita is still with me.
I'm hardly ever alone.

She brings food, she laughs
and sings, but even when
she's silent,

the rhythm of her breathing
sounds musical,

like a cool breeze of survival
in this forest of butterflies
and vultures.

THE FOREST

1907

THE HOWLER MONKEYS

GHOSTLY

WE KNOW DEATH

WE FEAR DEATH

WE SMELL DEATH

WE HATE DEATH

OUR VOICES RISE

FROM THE TREES

ABOVE EVERY

GRAVEYARD

OF STRANGERS

OUR VOICES

CHASE DEATH

AND STRANGERS

AWAY

GO

GO

GO

THE MOSQUITOES

THIRST

We drink blood

We need blood

We pierce skin

We swallow

Blood.

We fly to blood

We crawl to blood

We swim to blood

We need

Blood.

THE VAMPIRE BATS

HUNGER

We sleep in caves all day

leap into dark air at night

run and bound on the ground

follow the heat

of blood

in veins

follow the rhythm

of a sleeper's

breath

our teeth

shave fur

clip feathers

bite skin.

Any sleeping bird

beast

human

can fill

our hunger

as long as

there is

the heat

of blood.

THE VIOLET-GREEN SWALLOWS

SWOOPING

All evening in the sky

up and down

we dart

to gobble

mosquitoes

we swoop to escape

from the nets

of human hunters

who wear our glistening

colorful feathers

as decorations

on their plain

white hats.

THE TREES

IF ONLY

If we could move swiftly
we would run
leap
fly

but our only movement
is growth

less
and less
growth
after each sunrise
of dynamite explosions
and sharpened blades
of the ruthless
ax.

OPEN HOURS

1908

MATEO

LEARNING

My thoughts are still scattered
by weakness, but this recurring fever
is teaching me to value every breath,
and the luxury of surviving makes me long
to ask questions about my silver life . . .

Why do gold men who fall ill receive
sick pay, while I get nothing?

Will I ever be brave enough to run away
from my contract and risk being arrested
as a vagrant?

I don't want to end up with an iron collar
clamped around my neck, and an iron ball
dragged by a chain attached to the collar,
like those prisoners I sometimes see
working on the road gang.

HENRY

SO LITTLE TO GIVE

Each time the raging fever

overcomes Mateo, Anita delivers

quinine, and I share my food.

I'd love to offer more, but here

in this crate town, there's not much

to give.

So I pound on a tree-trunk drum,

and I sing silly songs to help

my friend laugh, once he's

well enough

to listen.

ANITA

VULNERABLE

When Mateo
is finally well enough
to return to his horrible job,
I'm alone,
so I climb a hill that offers
a spectacular view
of both oceans.

Mateo's illness
has left me frightened.

How little it takes to destroy
the life
of a person
or a mountain.

AUGUSTO

DEMOTED

Goethals has just announced

that he will purge all misfits

from the gold payroll.

By *misfits* he means dark men.

Black Americans. Panamanians.

Puerto Ricans. All of us hired

as exceptions

to the segregation

rules.

That era is over now.

Suddenly, we are silver men.

Silver housing.

Silver food.

A silver level

of hope.

MATEO

MOVING DAY

We help Augusto pack,
borrow a mule, lift crates of books,
tie bundles of paintings, and carry
his fragile curiosities—each bone,
feather, egg, statue, tusk, and horn
a scientific treasure, yet so strange,
as if we have filled whole boxes
with eerie shadows.

We help move him into a rustic room
at La Cubana María, the clinic-inn
where Anita grew up, and where she
and old María tend their marvelous
garden of cures.

Augusto seems comforted as he strolls
along the pathways, bending over one flower
after another, to enjoy the variety
of smells.

AUGUSTO

WHEN DOORS CLOSE

My days of luxury are over,

but I won't give in without

a protest.

I plan to challenge Goethals face to face,

man to man, just as the newspapers describe

when reporters write about his famous

"open hours," a time especially designated

for hearing the grievances

of ordinary workers.

So I climb the one thousand steep steps

of Canal Commission headquarters

that lead up to an imposing building,

where I wait in a stuffy hallway,

along with hundreds of other

furious,

grumbling,

cursing,

demoted men.

When my turn to be heard

finally comes, I'm sent to the office

of a minor undersecretary

who does not even pretend

to listen.

I should have known

that Goethals's "open hours"

would be open only

to gold men.

MATEO

UNREST

Rage spreads from demoted men
to anarchists, and then it spreads
all the way to gold men. Walkouts.
Sit-downs. Fistfights. Battles
with Canal Zone police.

When gold steam-shovel drivers
go out on strike, open hours
don't do them any good.

Goethals merely fires them and hires
new men, strikebreakers shipped in
from far away.

Even the gold nurses are threatening
to strike if Goethals persists in demanding
that they pay for seamstresses
to make their new uniforms.

HENRY

SKY PONDS

When I'm suddenly transferred
to a fumigation crew, I feel
as though I've been delivered
from misery.

No more digging. No more mud.
I receive a ladder and bucket,
a spray hose, the oil . . .

Climbing rung by rung, up, up, up,
to the crowns of tall trees, I begin
to see how impossible it will be
to spray every single puddle
in all of Panama.

Tiny pools of rain are trapped
at the bases of orchid leaves
and other air plants—flowers

that dangle from high branches,

their naked roots drinking

from drifting mist

instead of soil . . .

Sky ponds and air plants

are things I learned about by listening

to Augusto. Sometimes, science

seems just as mysterious

as church.

There are tadpoles in the sky ponds,

and mosquito larvae, and bright

blue frogs. I spray the oil on all

those creatures, watching them

vanish beneath a haze

of rainbow-glazed

death.

When lunchtime comes,

I climb down the ladder

rung by rung, and then

I lean that ladder

against a tree trunk,

and when a foreman shows me

where to line up for lunch,

I see that there aren't

any chairs or benches,

so I slip away

into the forest,

and I just keep

walking

and walking

until I'm gone.

MATEO

ONE DARING ESCAPE LEADS TO ANOTHER

After Henry disappears, I accept
la vieja María's invitation to move
out of the crate town, where police
are on the prowl, seeking
fugitives.

La Cubana María Inn is almost
empty. Big new American hotels
and hospitals are putting Anita's
adopted *abuelita* out of business,
but the old woman does not seem
too worried.

Instead, she sits down and visits,
telling tales and asking questions
about our shared homeland.

Remembering the island
makes me wistful.

I speak of places

I barely remember.

Places I visited with Mami,

before I started hiding

from Papi.

A zoo.

A park.

A café.

The beach.

Now I'm hiding again,

hiding from the police,

because I won't go back

to that track-moving,

backbreaking,

brain-shattering

culebra, cucaracha,

serpent, cockroach

cut, slide

hell.

AUGUSTO

NO ESCAPE

Perhaps I'm not as brave
as Henry and Mateo.

Or maybe it's just my foolish hope
that continuing to study and map
the ever-changing slopes
of the Serpent Cut
really might save
a few lives . . .

so I ride the labor train
down into mud, and at the end
of each workday, I ride it back,
and on Sundays, at last,
there's freedom,
exploration,
art, science,
wild wings . . .

HENRY

A NEW LIFE

Native villagers accept me.

I soon learn that the blue frogs

I saw in those sky ponds

are useful for poisoning

the sharp tips

of darts.

If I stay here, I'll have to learn

how to hunt with a blowgun,

and I'll learn to speak

a new language.

If I stay in this misty heat, I'll wear

hardly any clothes, and I'll paint

my skin with the juice of red

achiote berries to keep

biting mosquitoes

from killing me with fevers.

If I stay, I'll have to forget

that old dream of buying farmland

at home.

Home is here now.

Home is a hut propped on stilts,

as protection against floods

and crocodiles.

I try not to think of Momma,

waiting for a letter,

waiting for silver.

ANITA

MONKEY SCHOOL

This morning, a baby howler
slid down a branch and reached
for my hand with his small fingers.

It was a tender moment,
his face almost human,
the eyes so intelligent.

Now it's evening, and the little howler
has returned to his family, but I've
already made friends with another
funny monkey, a skinny capuchin,
like the ones that are chained
and trained by organ grinders
in Silver Town.

She sits in a leafy nest, sipping
from the wet fur of her long tail.
When the fur is dry, she dips

195

the tail into a sky pond

and sips one more time,

never descending low enough

to risk touching the river

where crocodiles

wait.

Quietly, the little monkey and I

sit together in a treetop, listening.

Learning.

THE FOREST

1908

ONE HOWLER MONKEY

TWO VOICES

I'M YOUNG, BUT I LEARN
HOW TO THROW MY NOISY VOICE
ACROSS TREETOPS, LIKE A CLOUD
OR A BIRD, REACHING FAR . . .

and then I reach down
with my arm, hand, knuckles,
fingertips, reaching just far enough
to touch
a stranger's hand,
a stranger's small,
quiet voice.

When I leap back up to my family,
I remember the human song,
AND I HOWL.

THE CAPUCHIN MONKEY

CLEVER

I'm small and smart

I know how to leap

or perch on a branch

dip my tail into a pond

sip

from the tip

of the fur

never risking

the muddy shore

where jaws

and teeth

lurk.

THE GIANT SWALLOWTAIL BUTTERFLIES

SALT

We're not afraid of slow, wide jaws.

We land on crocodile

or peccary

or tapir

skin,

nose,

eyes . . .

We need to sip

the salt of earth

wherever we find

minerals,

sweat,

tears.

THE KING VULTURE

DEATH

Death is king
in the mud
on steep slopes

Death is food
in the heat
in the rain

Death is life
in my beak
down my throat

Death in my belly
every day
all day.

THE TREES

LIFE

So many of us are gone now

that survivors

struggle

to grow
enough green

for hungry birds and monkeys
who leave our branches stripped
of leaves and twigs and fruit
even though we need
their help

to move
seeds . . .

THE CROCODILE BRIDGE

1910

MATEO

BIRD ART

Last year, Augusto finally
abandoned his contract.

He has made arrangements
to sell paintings of birds to museums
far away — my paintings along with his,
as if he understands that I am already
a true artist, capable of showing
the beauty of wild creatures
in flight.

I find it hard to believe
that in the old days, bird artists
killed their subjects, then stuffed
and posed them, instead of painting
life.

ANITA

UNCERTAINTY

Each sight in the forest is always new.

Mateo paints bellbirds, woodpeckers,

and shining honeycreepers,

while I climb massive ceiba trees

with buttress roots

so immense that they look

like stone fortresses,

and then I climb walking trees

with skinny

stilt roots

that make

them look

like dancers.

All of it seems so permanent, until

we pass through areas where logging

has left nothing but mud, dust, mud . . .

MATEO

FOREST NIGHTS

At dusk, there's the blinking flash
of fireflies and the steady light
of phosphorescent mushrooms.

Together, Anita and I wonder
how anything as ordinary
as an insect, or a fungus,
can glow
in the dark.

Will every detail of nature
always seem
so mysterious?

HENRY

LOVE IS A NEW LANGUAGE

I have found my own sweet sweet
bride. I'm going to marry a village girl
from the Emberá tribe.

No one from the Serpent Cut ever
thinks about the native people
who truly belong to this butterfly forest.

No one wonders what Panama was like
before the logging, digging, hauling,
and landslides . . .

but now, so many islanders have run away
from silver jobs that languages are blending—
English, Spanish, and French, all mixed up
with Chibchan and Chocó.

It's as if we're creating an entirely
new culture.

MATEO

VISITING HENRY

The *indios* live in open huts
without walls, each floor a platform
propped up on stilts, high above
rainy-season floods
and roaming crocodiles.

If a notched log leans against
the side of a thatched hut, I know
that strangers are welcome to climb up
and visit, but if the log ladder lies flat
on the ground, Anita and I walk on quietly
while villagers sleep
in their peacefully
swaying
hammocks.

The roofs are dry palm fronds,
the floors covered with woven reeds.
Faces are painted with red and black

designs — circles and looped lines

made from insect-repelling *bixa* juice.

On feast days, Henry joins the village men

as they dance, wearing headdresses

and capes of leaves that make them look

like green birds as they twirl

and leap,

carrying

human prayers

up toward heaven.

Quickly, I sketch each movement

of the dance, hoping to paint

the bright details

later.

So much of life and art

requires patience.

Will any painting ever

feel complete?

HARRY FRANCK

from the United States of America

Census Enumerator

COUNTING

I came to Panama planning to dig
the Eighth Wonder of the World,
but I was told that white men
should never be seen working
with shovels, so I took a police job,
and now I've been transferred
to the census.

I roam the jungle, counting laborers
who live in shanties and those who live
on the run, fugitives who are too angry
to keep working for silver in a system
where they know that others
earn gold.

When islanders see me coming,
they're afraid of trouble, even though

I can't arrest them anymore—now
all I need is a record of their names, ages,
homelands, and colors.

The rules of this census confound me.
I'm expected to count white Jamaicans
as dark and every shade of Spaniard
as semi-white, so that Americans
can pretend
there's only one color
in each country.

How am I supposed to enumerate
this kid with the Cuban accent?
His skin is medium, but his eyes
are green.

And what about that Puerto Rican
scientist, who speaks like a New York
professor,
or the girl who says she doesn't know
where she was born or who her parents

are—she could be part native, or part French,
Jamaican, Chinese . . .

She could even be part American,
from people who passed through here
way back
in gold rush days.

Counting feels just as impossible
as turning solid mountains
into a ditch.

ANITA

COUNTLESS

No category.

I don't fit.

No box.

No shape.

No space

for me

in the census enumerator's

tidy columns

of numbers.

No mark.

No label.

No tag I can wear

that states "enumerated"

and names

my color.

For the first time in my life, I love

being unknown.

MATEO

PAYING WITH MUSIC

I wear my enumerated tag only
for a few minutes,
until the counting man
vanishes from view,
hidden by tangled vines,
and strangler figs, and taunting,
howling, shrieking monkeys.

At Henry's village wedding, all the drums
and dancing are festive, like a memory
of rhythmic island waves, island shores . . .
For just a moment, I feel a flash of wishing.
After I fled, was Papi happy?

You owe me a song, Henry shouts
as he dances, reminding me
that silver men have nothing else
to give and runaway silver men
have even less.

So I lift my rackety, clattering voice,

and as it joins Anita's

smoothly flowing melody,

our combined song feels

like a gift received,

instead of given.

AUGUSTO

POSSIBILITIES

Seeing Henry happy and free
and young Mateo so wildly in love,
I start wondering if I will ever
be the settle-down, quiet-down
marrying type.

For now, all I want is exploration.
Painting. Keeping a record of wings,
eggs, and nests, to preserve the beauty
of rare creatures, before this
not-so-impossible-after-all canal
finally floods the entire
butterfly forest.

On paper and canvas, anything
can happen.

Motionless wings spring to life
on museum walls, convincing

generous strangers

in distant cities

that funds must be raised

to create permanent refuges

where trees, flowers, birds, frogs,

mushrooms, and monkeys

stand a chance of survival.

That's all I plead for—just a chance—

when I write fervent letters to Roosevelt,

whose presidency has ended, so that now

he devotes all his energy to saving

wilderness. He's become a champion

of national parks and an amateur explorer

as well—I've even heard that he's planning

his own scientific expedition

to the Amazon.

Sometimes, life changes so suddenly

that the future is like a curiosity cabinet,

filled with surprises.

MATEO

MEN REPLACED BY METAL

News from the Serpent Cut
is carried by alarmed travelers.

A train-track-shifting machine
has been invented.

Only nine men are needed
to operate the huge crane car.

Six hundred Spaniards
have abruptly been fired.

The jobs they hated
are gone.

MATEO

RAVENOUS

Fired men roam the jungle,
searching for jobs to earn money
for fare back to Cuba or back
to their own native provinces
in Spain.

Hungry and angry, drunk anarchists
spend their last silver wages on rum

instead of food, so that one evening
when Anita and I are out collecting
herbs, we learn that silver people
can be just as cruel
as gold.

On a swaying rope bridge
above a river churning with crocodiles,
three of my old boxcar roommates
stand blurry-eyed and laughing

as they toss a fighting rooster
down, into the thrashing mass
of ravenous reptiles.

Twisting and snapping, the jaws
of crocodiles gape, rip, and gulp,
as each one seizes a share of the
helpless bird.

A single red feather rises
from the mess, floating like a flag
in a war zone . . .

while Anita steps forward to explain
that the hungry beasts will grow
accustomed to associating humans
with food and they'll go hunting
upstream, in villages where they'll
kill and eat chickens, goats, dogs,
or children.

ANITA

WITNESS

Angry people never listen—

all they want is action—

so they ignore me,

and they grab Mateo,

and they lift him, trying to toss him

over the whipping, snapping, swaying

ropes.

MATEO

TEETERING

For one horrifying instant,
I feel as if I'm already over the edge
of the perilous rope bridge . . .

but it's just a bounce
in midair
before I fall back down
to safety,
rescued by brave Anita,
who flourishes her machete,
chasing the mean men
away,
far
away . . .

ANITA

STORM

Alone in the forest again,

we're surrounded by beauty

and danger,

soaring wings,

screeching cries,

whirling wind,

lightning, thunder, a cloudburst,

and howls, our own powerful

voices . . .

THE FOREST

1910

THE HOWLER MONKEYS

ALARM

WHEN STRANGERS RUN BELOW US

WE HOWL HOOT WHOOP BOOM

CHASE CHASE CHASE

WITH OUR VOICES

WE LEAP

FROM TREE TO TREE

WE KNOW

OUR VOICES ARE STRONG

CLAWS OF AIR

FANGS OF SOUND

GO

GO

GO

THE SCARLET MACAWS

ALARM

We fly

Screech

Call

To one another

As we fly

Soar

Cry

Flap

Clatter

Chatter

Escape

With our wild

FREEDOM

We fly

THE POISON DART FROGS

ALARM

we love to sing

for mates

but now we sing

from fear

our warning

to one another

unseen

hidden

by leaves

we sing sing sing

climb climb climb

hiding our voices

in trees

THE TREES

ALARM

A wind of voices
the storm of warnings

hot crackles of lightning
explosions of thunder

fierce splinters
of flame

then our whisper
rain
rain.

SKY CASTLES
1914

MATEO AND ANITA TOGETHER

WHEN MOUNTAINS BECOME ISLANDS

Last year, when all the digging finally ended,
this entire forest was flooded—trees drowned,
crate towns vanished, and at least
fifty thousand silver people
had to flee for their lives,
along with native villagers
and all the wildlife, including
desperately swimming jaguars
and flailing, hooting, howling
monkeys . . .

Even the birds
lost their nests.

Only this one mountain peak survived.
It's an island now—our new home.

We have a stilt hut on a slope
high above the water,

and we've built a terrace

we think of as our sky castle,

because it overlooks dangling

air plants

and tiny sky ponds

in soaring treetops.

Squeaks, roars, plumes of scent,

the drumming beaks of toucans,

the waving-leg signals of golden frogs

as they talk to one another in their own

amphibious sign language . . .

so many unique ways

to communicate.

Our only way of speaking

with the forest

is silence.

We watch. We study. We record

all that we see as we peer

into hummingbird nests
and howler eyes.

We listen.

We've counted as many as forty species
of rare and common birds
in a single tree when the wild figs
are ripe.

We sketch, paint, and hope to remember
every detail of beauty.

237

We keep a shared journal
as we gather medicinal herbs
for distant museums that want to include
every plant in the world in their vast
scientific collections.

Sometimes, we feel like strangers,
and at other times, we feel
transformed

into a natural part
of this wild
world.

When Augusto visits, he brings excited
explorers from all the distant cities
where he sells our paintings
and herbs.

The canal has sliced this nation
in half, so when Henry comes visiting—
along with his growing family of lively
children—they have to cross the water
on a ferry, then row a canoe
across the huge man-made lake
called Gatún, a lake that was created
to slow the rapids of the Chagres River
in order to fill enormous
concrete boxes called locks,
which are used as a way
to float huge ships

up from one ocean's sea level

to another.

Both Augusto and Henry were here

when we got married in a green aisle

of trees, with a singing red macaw

as our best man and a chattering

capuchin monkey

as bridesmaid.

We dream of someday studying

at one of the faraway colleges

where our work is displayed

on gallery walls,

but for now,

we have only a single goal:

learning to understand

this one mountain-island

of massive roots,

delicate wings,

and huge voices

that croak, squawk, shriek,

chant, whistle, and howl

about hunger,

freedom,

danger,

and love,

always love.

THE FOREST

1914

THE HOWLER MONKEYS

AT REST

MIDDAY
NO DANGEROUS
STRANGERS
JUST SILENCE
HEAT
SHADE
SLEEP
DREAMS
OF HOWLING
AT THUNDER
HOWLING
AT WIND
HOWLING
AT RAIN
HOWLING
STRENGTH
HOWLING
HOPE

THE RESPLENDENT QUETZAL

CAMOUFLAGE

Nest in a hole in a tree

Eggs

Then hungry hatchlings

Flight

From below in midair I swoop

And I pluck tasty fruit

My feathers the same shiny green

As leafy branches

Safe from the laughing falcon

High above

Ha ha ha

Safe

Back in the nest

In a hole in a tree

Only my long tail exposed

Leafy green.

POISON DART TADPOLES

SWIMMING

blue on forest mud

our father wrestles

with other males

blue on forest mud

our father protects us

from fire-bellied snakes

blue on forest mud

our father lifts us onto his back

and carries us one at a time

up a tall tree

into a sky pond

blue on forest mud

our mother climbs up

to visit us

swimming.

THE TREES

HOME

Everything lives on us or under us

Everything needs

Wood

Leaves

Flowers

Fruit

Seeds

Even the rain needs our roots

In deep mud

Water absorbed

Lifted

Released

From our green

Water transformed into mist

Clouds

More rain

New growth

Home

No matter how small home

Has become

Just a mountaintop island

Our home

Steady growth.

EPILOGUE

HOWL!

Mateo, Anita, Henry—

Greetings from the Panama-Pacific International Exposition in San Francisco. Visitors from all over the world are here, touring miniature replicas of the canal's engineering marvels. The tourists are astonished as they gaze at reproductions of a man-made Wonder of the World that is being called the "kiss of the oceans," represented by colorful pictures of two mermaids meeting for the first time. Tourists are thrilled by cultural exhibits from continents newly joined by the watery shortcut: Europe, Asia, Africa, Australia, and the Americas, both North and South.

I can hardly understand it, but you must believe me: There is not a single exhibit honoring silver people. No songs or dances from the Caribbean islands where most of us were recruited. Not even one booth showing the daily lives of all the brave laborers who accomplished the impossible task of digging with nothing but shovels and courage. There are no monuments honoring the tens of thousands who died in Serpent Cut mud.

No one cares. No one cares because no one knows. If our history is ever to be told, we must tell it ourselves. Like howlers in the forest, we must lift our voices above the noise of thunder and dynamite.

Dear friends, *amigos queridos*, write your memories; help me howl our wild truth.

Augusto

California, 1915

HISTORICAL NOTE

I grew up in Los Angeles during the 1960s. My family marched for civil rights, singing "We Shall Overcome," but when my Cuban mother described the need for equality, she spoke of Panama more often than Mississippi. Like most Latin Americans, she was far more familiar with Canal Zone apartheid than Jim Crow laws. Many years later, as a botanist collecting wild plants in Central America's rainforests, I had the chance to meet descendants of "silver people" from Jamaica. This book is a small gesture of thanks for their friendliness and hospitality.

Silver People is a work of historical fiction, set in factual situations, in real places. There really was an inn called La Cubana María. The Culebra (Serpent) Cut became known as the Gaillard Cut. The mountain that became an island is Barro Colorado, maintained by the Smithsonian Tropical Research Institute as one of the world's most thoroughly studied remnants of rainforest. Mateo, Henry, Anita, Old María, and Augusto are imaginary characters. John Stevens, Theodore Roosevelt, George Goethals, Jackson Smith, Gertrude Beeks, and Harry Franck are historical figures. Poems in the voices of historical figures are based on their own documented statements.

The importation of laborers from the Caribbean islands to Panama began during the California gold rush, when a railroad was built by Americans as an alternative to mule trains. A Cuban American engineer named Aniceto Menocal surveyed possible routes for a U.S. canal project, but France was the first nation to actually try digging. The disastrous French attempt lasted throughout the 1880s, shattered France's economy, and sacrificed the lives of more than twenty-two thousand laborers. In 1903, the United States backed a military coup that separated the province of Panama from the nation of Colombia. In exchange, Panama granted permission for a project that lasted ten years. Beginning in 1904, laborers were once again imported, and another fifty-six hundred lives were lost to yellow fever, malaria, and landslides. The canal was completed by a conglomerate of U.S. government and business interests called the Isthmian Canal Commission. Workers from more than one hundred countries participated, but the vast majority were Caribbean islanders, primarily English-speaking Jamaicans and Barbadians. On the island of Cuba, American recruiters specifically hired American military nurses and "semi-white" Spaniards, many of whom turned out to be active members of an anarchist movement.

In the American-ruled Canal Zone, laborers from all over the world were subjected to a system that resembled South Africa's apartheid. Dark-skinned islanders and olive-skinned southern Europeans were paid in silver. Light-skinned Americans and northern Europeans received gold. Housing, meals, recreation, and hospitals were also strictly segregated.

Of the estimated quarter-million Caribbean islanders who worked in Panama between 1850 and 1914, at least one-third never returned to their homelands but fanned out across Central America, becoming an integral part of the region's rich cultural heritage.

The canal was intended as a link between continents, as well as a way to shorten shipping routes. The Panama Canal's opening ceremony was planned as a festive celebration of worldwide prosperity and peace, but the month was August 1914. With the outbreak of World War I, the first ship to pass through the canal was a U.S. military vessel, on its way to Europe's battlefields.

The discriminatory silver/gold payroll system continued until 1955. Possession of the Canal Zone was ceded to Panama in 1979, but operation of the canal was not transferred from the United States to Panama until the eve of the year 2000.

Eventual opening of wider modern shipping lanes will be linked to the expansion of key U.S. ports, allowing continued passage of increasingly enormous container ships from China. This time, the digging is being accomplished by heavy equipment, rather than imported labor.

Strange as it seems, the "globalization" of international trade did not begin with the Internet but was launched a century ago, when a new waterway suddenly made the world seem small.

Margarita Engle
California, 2014

SELECTED REFERENCES

Maps of Panama can be found on this site:
ian.macky.net/pat/map/pa/pa.html

Franck, Harry A. *Zone Policeman 88.* New York: Century, 1920.

Greene, Julie. *The Canal Builders.* New York: Penguin, 2009.

James, Winifred. *The Mulberry Tree.* London: Chapman, 1913.

Keller, Ulrich. *The Building of the Panama Canal in Historic Photographs.* New York: Dover, 1983.

Mabrey, Gerardo. *El Canal de Panamá y los trabajadores antillanos.* Panama City: Universidad de Panamá, 1989.

McGuinness, Aims. *Path of Empire.* Ithaca, N.Y.: Cornell University Press, 2008.

Newton, Velma. *The Silver Men.* Kingston, Jamaica: University of the West Indies, 1984.

Parker, Matthew. *Panama Fever.* New York: Anchor, 2009.

Rivas Reyes, Marcela Eyra. *El trabajo de las mujeres en la historia de la construcción del Canal de Panamá (1881–1914).* Panama City: Universidad de Panamá, 2002.

Russell, Carlos E. *An Old Woman Remembers: The Recollected History of West Indians in Panama, 1855–1955.* Brooklyn: Caribbean Diaspora Press, 1995.

Seacole, Mary. *Wonderful Adventures of Mrs. Seacole in Many Lands.* New York: Penguin, 2005.

Serra, Yolanda Marco. *Los obreros españoles en la construcción del Canal de Panamá.* Portobelo, Panamá: 1907.

ACKNOWLEDGMENTS

I thank God for tropical rainforests.

The following resources were helpful:

Isthmian Historical Society

Panama Collection of the Canal Zone
Library-Museum

Silver People Heritage Foundation

Smithsonian Tropical Research Institute

United States National Archives

Central California Caribbean Association

For a thrilling wildlife tour of Barro Colorado Island, *gracias a* Vilma *y los monos aulladores* (the
howlers).

Special thanks to nonfiction wizard Angelica
Carpenter for advice about the mysteries of research
and to Ragina Shearer for suggesting that I give trees a
voice. For visions of bird art and sky castles, I am in-
debted to the paintings of Louis A. Fuertes and the expedition diaries of Frank M. Chapman.

259

For encouragement and companionship, joyful hugs to my family. Special thanks to Victor, Kristan, and Jacob for dog-sitting.

Deep gratitude to my wonderful editor, Reka Simonsen. At times, this book seemed impossible. Without your insight, it would have been a muddy mess at best. I am also grateful to Lisa DiSarro, Elizabeth Tardiff, Susan Buckheit, and everyone else at HMH for true teamwork.